THE ZELL STANDARD

"LESSONS FROM A SELF-MADE BILLIONAIRE REAL ESTATE MOGUL SAM ZELL"

JAMERS JJD. JORDAN

TABLE OF CONTENTS

CHAPTER 1 5

THE EARLY YEARS 5

Sub-chapter 1.1: Humble Beginnings: Growing Up in Chicago 5

Sub-chapter 1.2: Entrepreneurial Sparks: First Ventures 11

CHAPTER 2 20

BREAKING INTO REAL ESTATE 20

Sub-chapter 2.1: The First Deals: Learning the Market 20

Sub-chapter 2.2: Building Equity Group Investments 27

CHAPTER 3 39

THE CONTRARIAN APPROACH 39

Sub-chapter 3.1: Buying When Others Sell: The Value of Distressed Assets 39

Sub-chapter 3.2: Risk and Reward: Calculated Decisions 48

CHAPTER 4 59

EXPANDING THE EMPIRE 59

Sub-chapter 4.1: Diversification Beyond Real Estate 59

Sub-chapter 4.2: Global Reach: Investing Overseas 67

CHAPTER 5 78

NAVIGATING CRISES AND DOWNTURNS 78

Sub-chapter 5.1: Surviving the 1990s Real Estate Crash 78

Sub-chapter 5.2: The Great Recession: A Strategic Response 85

CHAPTER 6 95

LEADERSHIP AND CORPORATE CULTURE 95

Sub-chapter 6.1: Building Teams: The Importance of Talent and Culture 95

Sub-chapter 6.2: Leading by Example: The Art of Direct Communication . 102

CHAPTER 7 109

THE ZELL LEGACY 109

Sub-chapter 7.1: Philanthropy and Giving Back 109

Sub-chapter 7.2: The Blueprint for Future Entrepreneurs 118

CHAPTER 1

THE EARLY YEARS

Sub-chapter 1.1: Humble Beginnings: Growing Up in Chicago

Sam Zell, also known as Shmuel Zielonka, was born on September 28, 1941, to Jewish immigrant parents who escaped from Poland right before World War II started.

His parents, Ruchla and Berek Zielonka managed to reach the United States in 1939, barely avoiding the Holocaust that would inflict significant damage on their homeland.

The family made Chicago their home, a city famous for its lively communities and abundant chances, where Sam's father started fresh as a wholesale jeweler. Zell's character and entrepreneurial mindset were profoundly influenced by the immigrant experience and the resilience of his parents.

Zell's parents' escape story reflects great courage and strength. Following a challenging expedition across Siberia, Japan, and Canada, they ultimately reached the United States with little more than a strong determination to begin anew.

Sam was deeply affected by the trauma of leaving his homeland and losing numerous loved ones, driving him to maximize his chances.

Being raised in a family of immigrants post-World War II allowed him to witness the sacrifices his parents made and the importance they placed on education, diligence, and persistence.

Residing in a mostly Jewish area on the North Side of Chicago, young Sam grew up in a tight-knit community that upheld cultural traditions and fostered a strong sense of identity.

His father, a resolute and creative man, frequently recounted tales of their departure from Poland and the wisdom gained from beginning a fresh life in a foreign country.

These narratives were not mere anecdotes; they served as instructional aids that molded Sam's perception of risk, reward, and the quest for independence. The family's experiences led to the development of a resilient mindset, which became a fundamental aspect of Zell's business philosophy.

Even though the family had limited financial resources, Zell's parents valued education highly and saw it as a path to a better future.

Sam's dad, a very intelligent man, was proficient in multiple languages and had a strong passion for politics, history, and literature.

This setting encouraged Sam's inquisitiveness and drive to compete, traits that would be crucial in his future as an entrepreneur. Sam's father's confidence in the American dream and the possibilities in a free market economy shaped Sam's ambition and fearless actions, a mindset that would characterize his business endeavors for many years.

Sam Zell had his first introduction to the business world at a young age. During his youth, he demonstrated a strong desire to earn money by selling comic books, purchasing and reselling fireworks, and doing various tasks within the community.

His talent for discovering methods to make money was clear from a young age, demonstrating a natural tendency towards business and starting businesses.

This independent mindset distinguished him from his colleagues, leading to a lifelong dedication to entrepreneurship.

Chicago, with its vibrant markets, varied neighborhoods, and thriving businesses, provided the perfect environment for Zell to nurture his entrepreneurial drive.

The strong real estate market, thriving industrial zones, and diverse culture of the city provided him with a range of business opportunities and strategies.

Watching the victories and setbacks of nearby companies, such as his father's wholesale jewelry business, gave him valuable insights that would shape his future investment tactics.

Sub-chapter 1.2: Entrepreneurial Sparks: First Ventures

Sam Zell's entrepreneurial venture truly started when he was studying law at the University of Michigan. Despite Zell's law studies, his real passions were outside the legal realm.

It was during college that he initially displayed his business skills by overseeing several small yet successful projects.

One of his initial business ventures included selling Playboy magazines to classmates—a business that expanded rapidly thanks to Zell's creative strategy.

He was able to dominate the market on campus by meeting the strong demand college students had for the magazine, despite their difficulty in obtaining it. His initial endeavors extended beyond magazines. Zell quickly broadened his involvement by overseeing student housing units.

He began by assisting a landlord in handling a small property and gradually assumed additional duties, eventually supervising multiple apartment complexes.

Zell showed a talent for boosting operational efficiencies, raising rents, and decreasing vacancies, abilities that would prove crucial in his later real estate success.

Succeeding in this endeavor showed him the profitable possibilities in real estate and confirmed his choice to explore non-traditional career paths, other than practicing law. Managing properties improved Zell's real estate skills and enhanced his grasp of risk and reward.

Unlike most of his contemporaries who chose traditional career paths, Zell flourished in the unpredictability of entrepreneurship, where each choice could lead to either success or failure.

He soon discovered that taking strategic risks was essential for achieving substantial rewards, a valuable lesson that would influence his professional journey.

His talent for recognizing potential in situations that appeared risky or uncertain became a characteristic that set him apart.

After he finished college in 1966, Zell opted out of a conventional legal profession and instead joined forces with his fraternity buddy, Robert Lurie.

Together, they established the beginnings of Equity Group Investments, a real estate investment company that would expand into a multi-billion-dollar business.

Zell and Lurie's initial collaboration was founded on a mutual desire for risk-taking and a readiness to defy conventional norms.

Their initial transactions included purchasing real estate in Midwestern college towns, where Zell noticed a need for student housing that was not being addressed.

The pair's plan was straightforward yet successful: purchase undervalued properties, refurbish them, and then rent them out at increased prices.

This model was successful and enabled Zell to rapidly expand by acquiring bigger and more intricate properties.

Renovating and managing these properties gave him a profound insight into the real estate market, from evaluating deals to navigating property management complexities.

It solidified his tendency to go against the norm, as he frequently sought out opportunities in underestimated or neglected markets.

Zell's initial projects set the foundation for his upcoming business approach, prioritizing recognizing undervalued assets, making quick decisions, and having a strong sense of worth.

His tenure at the University of Michigan was not only about academics; it was a crucial time when he grasped the significance of entrepreneurship, acquired skills to make the best of chances, and honed his ability to spot undervalued assets.

The basic teachings and his immigrant heritage were the building blocks for Zell's success as a billionaire who made his fortune.

Even in his youth as an entrepreneur, Zell was already distinguishing himself by utilizing overlooked strategies.

Even though most investors avoided distressed assets or troubled markets, Zell found potential in challenging situations.

His skill in handling difficult scenarios, coupled with his determination to work hard, enabled him to take advantage of chances that were overlooked by others.

This method would be a defining characteristic of his professional life, leading to him being known as "the Grave Dancer" because he often identified worth in businesses and properties others considered worthless.

Zell's career was significantly shaped by his early experiences in Chicago and his first entrepreneurial ventures at the University of Michigan.

The core values of his immigrant parents, including perseverance, self-reliance, and respect for freedom, helped him navigate the challenges of his initial business endeavors.

Upon graduating from college, Zell had already established the groundwork for a business mindset that would propel him to become one of the top real estate investors globally.

From a young boy selling comic books in Chicago to a college student managing real estate, his journey demonstrates the strength of resilience and the drive of entrepreneurship. In the years ahead, Zell would further develop the knowledge gained in his youth, creating a career characterized by daring choices, thoughtful risk management, and a readiness to question traditional beliefs.

The entrepreneurial interest that started in college would soon develop into a strong passion, pushing him toward success and changing the real estate industry.

The beginning of Sam Zell's life offers a glimpse into how a billionaire was created and shows how a son of immigrants from Chicago could reach the top of American business with determination and a sharp sense of opportunity.

CHAPTER 2

BREAKING INTO REAL ESTATE

Sub-chapter 2.1: The First Deals: Learning the Market

Sam Zell did not make a big, planned entrance into the real estate industry; instead, he made strategic decisions that showed his talent for identifying opportunities in situations that others viewed as risky.

After graduating from the University of Michigan in 1966, Zell chose not to pursue a typical legal career. Instead, he decided to enter the real estate industry, which had captivated him while he was overseeing student housing in college.

Zell's initial investments were modest, mainly concentrated on residential properties in college towns in the Midwest, where he had already seen high demand for student housing.

His initial transaction was a humble one: purchasing a tiny apartment complex close to the University of Michigan. Zell noticed the property's potential, but it was not performing well because of inadequate management and maintenance.

While working at student apartments in college, he discovered that minor adjustments in property management could result in notable value boosts.

Taking this into consideration, he and Robert Lurie purchased the building at a reduced price and made improvements like fresh paint, upgraded lighting, and better services for tenants. The outcomes were nearly instant: the occupancy rate rose, rents went up, and the property value experienced significant growth.

Zell learned several key real estate investing lessons from these early experiences. Initially, the significance of recognizing underpriced assets was evident.

He discovered that properties facing difficulties or with problems in management frequently offered the best chances for increasing value.

The objective was to see beyond the superficial issues and recognize the possibility for enhancement. For Zell, the focus was not solely on purchasing items at a low cost but rather on locating assets where he could enhance value through operational enhancements or strategic changes.

Next, Zell promptly discovered that his ability to comprehend market trends and make quick decisions would be crucial for his success.

The real estate market experienced significant fluctuations due to frequent changes in demand and property values.

Zell's tendency to go against the norm, shaped by his immigrant family's history of resilience and survival, prompted him to embrace risks that others shied away from. Instead of following the crowd by investing in popular markets and properties, Zell preferred to target secondary markets and neglected assets, convinced that they offered greater potential for growth with proper management.

A difficult early investment for Zell was a transaction related to a commercial property in downtown Chicago. The building was old, with a lot of empty units and cheap rents.

Compared to the student housing projects, this commercial property necessitated more advanced management and significant capital upgrades. Zell decided to take a chance, thinking that by making the right improvements, the property could entice more desirable renters and demand increased rental fees.

Nevertheless, the plan did not unfold as expected. The renovations exceeded the expected timeline, went over budget, and struggled to find tenants.

Zell dealt with financial challenges that impacted his resources and led him to reconsider his strategy. However, rather than withdrawing, he adjusted, taking the experience as a valuable lesson in the intricacies of commercial real estate.

He discovered that some properties cannot be quickly transformed and that the timing of market conditions is essential for investment success. This lesson showed him the value of always having a safety buffer in his investments and emphasized the significance of thorough research and managing expenses.

Zell viewed the setbacks as valuable learning experiences, not failures. He improved his investment approach, concentrating on properties with a clear potential for growth and making sure he had the necessary resources and skills to carry out his plans successfully.

This strategy became a signature of his investment strategy: underpriced purchase assets, enhance their value, and subsequently either keep them for consistent income or sell them for a gain.

This method of value-added investing became the basis of Zell's career and was a strategy he used in different industries outside of real estate.

Sub-chapter 2.2: Building Equity Group Investments

In the late 1960s, Zell's interest in real estate continued to expand. After completing a few profitable transactions, he understood that to expand his business, he required a structured investment system capable of managing more deals.

In 1968, Zell and his longtime partner Robert Lurie established Equity Group Investments (EGI). EGI began as a tiny investment company specializing in real estate purchases but soon grew into a multi-billion-dollar corporation. Zell and Lurie's different abilities were essential for EGI's expansion.

Zell was responsible for making deals and strategizing, while Lurie handled the financial aspects of managing the firm's capital structure.

EGI's original approach was straightforward yet successful: procure troubled or underestimated properties, enhance their administration, and then capitalize on the profits.

Zell believed in consistently seeking out opportunities others overlooked, a tactic that distinguished him from typical real estate investors. During the late 1960s and early 1970s, EGI concentrated mainly on residential and commercial properties in the Midwest, where Zell possessed a deep understanding of the market dynamics.

These areas were frequently ignored by investors from the East Coast and West Coast, who chose to invest in the thriving markets of New York, Los Angeles, and San Francisco.

Zell recognized the potential in this opening and took advantage of it.

In the 1970s, EGI started to vary its investment holdings by branching out from residential properties to include industrial and commercial real estate.

This was a tactical decision based on Zell's conviction in diversification as a protection against market fluctuations. Even though residential real estate had the potential to generate consistent income, the profits were typically restricted.

Commercial and industrial properties, however, provided greater potential profits, though accompanied by greater dangers.

EGI aimed to diversify its portfolio by including various property types to stabilize the company's revenue and minimize risk from specific market sectors.

EGI experienced a significant shift in the mid-1970s, thanks to Zell noticing a huge potential in the industrial industry. The American economy was experiencing fluctuation because of the oil crisis, increased inflation, and higher interest rates. The economic difficulties resulted in a decline in the industrial real estate sector, prompting numerous property owners to offer significant discounts for sale.

Despite the economic uncertainty causing hesitation among many investors, Zell recognized the potential value of industrial properties.

He concluded that with the economy improving, there would be a rise in demand for industrial spaces, causing property values and rents to go up.

During this time, EGI energetically purchased industrial properties, building up a large collection that would later bring in substantial profits when the market improved.

Zell's skill in long-term thinking and predicting market cycles was evident in the successful industrial investments made by EGI.

He was not only responding to the present market situation but also preparing the company for future profits. EGI's investment strategy was defined by a contrarian approach that included purchasing when others were selling and selling when others were buying.

A deep comprehension of market basics was necessary, as well as the bravery to challenge the current market opinion.

As EGI expanded, Zell further diversified the firm's investments beyond just real estate. In the 1980s, EGI had transformed into a varied investment firm, with stakes in energy, transportation, manufacturing, and media.

Zell believed that the principles of value investing extended beyond just real estate, leading the firm to expand into other industries.

He recognized the potential in troubled assets in different industries and utilized EGI's resources to realize that value.

Zell's skill in attracting and keeping top talent was a crucial factor in EGI's growth strategy. He realized that expanding the business involved not only money, but also a group of experienced professionals capable of handling intricate transactions, overseeing properties, and navigating regulatory landscapes. Zell's leadership style was characterized by being hands-on yet empowering.

He nurtured a company environment that promoted creativity, acknowledged achievement, and accepted strategic risk.

This setting appealed to individuals with similar philosophies who flourished under Zell's guidance, enabling EGI to expand quickly and adjust to evolving market circumstances.

EGI's competitive advantage was also strengthened by its capacity to carry out intricate transactions. Zell and his team gained expertise in arranging deals that utilized different financial tools, such as debt, equity, and partnerships.

This financial strategy enabled EGI to increase profits while reducing risk, which was especially successful during times of economic uncertainty.

Zell's ability to organize deals and secure funds played a key role in the company's expansion, allowing EGI to seize opportunities that needed significant financial backing.

Towards the conclusion of the 1980s, EGI had solidified its status as a top investment company with a wide range of assets in its portfolio. The company achieved success not only because of the real estate market's growth, but also because of Zell's skill in recognizing value where others didn't, his readiness to take calculated risks, and his dedication to creating a team that could bring his vision to life.

These principles set the foundation for upcoming projects, such as establishing the public real estate investment trusts (REITs) that would become synonymous with Zell's career in the 1990s.

The strong base established in EGI's initial stages would benefit Zell greatly as he further grew his business realm.

The insights gained from his initial transactions—creating value, understanding market shifts, and managing risks—played a key role in forming the company's expansion plan. EGI's growth from a small real estate investment business to a multi-billion-dollar investment company showcased Zell's entrepreneurial drive, strategic planning, and determination to seize opportunities in various sectors.

While progressing, Zell would stick to the principles that had brought him success: purchasing low prices, selling them at high prices, and constantly searching for undervalued opportunities.

These principles and his tendency to think differently from others would result in some of his most significant achievements and occasional failures in the future. The early expansion of EGI is more than just about property; it's about an entrepreneur's vision to spot opportunities across the market and take advantage of them without hesitation.

CHAPTER 3

THE CONTRARIAN APPROACH

Sub-chapter 3.1: Buying When Others Sell: The Value of Distressed Assets

Throughout his career, Sam Zell is frequently known as a contrarian investor, a title he has fully accepted.

His investment strategy is centered on going against the mainstream by purchasing assets when others are keen to offload them and steering clear of the excitement during periods of overly positive market sentiment.

Zell's accomplishment in real estate and other sectors is mostly credited to his contrarian mindset, which guided him to invest in troubled assets, especially during economic crises. He recognized potential in places others saw danger, taking advantage of properties and companies with potential for high profits.

Zell's strategy towards troubled assets was based on a core belief: market fluctuations typically result in temporary discrepancies in value, rather than lasting decreases.

During times of fear and uncertainty among investors, asset prices often dropped below their true value, presenting chances for knowledgeable investors who could endure the situation.

Zell's strategy was to find these situations, assess the actual value of the assets, and purchase them at a reduced price. He frequently mentioned that his greatest interest in buying was when a business or real estate was unpopular or not in demand.

During the 1970s, the U.S. real estate market was severely affected by high inflation, increasing interest rates, and economic stagnation, in one of the earliest and most significant instances of this strategy in action.

Despite other investors being cautious about real estate due to uncertainty, Zell recognized a chance.

He thought the future demand for industrial, commercial, and residential properties would improve in the long run, despite the current gloomy outlook. His plan involved purchasing properties for low prices, enhancing their management, and retaining them until the market improved.

One key element of Zell's strategy was his skill in recognizing properties that had the potential to be repositioned or repurposed to generate additional value.

For instance, he purchased properties with high vacancy rates or management issues, confident that these problems could be solved with the appropriate strategy.

The important thing was to locate assets that had strong fundamentals, such as good locations, strong potential demand, and structural soundness, but were currently facing temporary challenges.

Zell frequently experienced substantial gains by enhancing these characteristics and being patient for the market to bounce back.

Zell's experience in the 1970s paved the way for even more daring actions in the decades that followed.

During the 1980s, he shifted his focus to office buildings, which were experiencing an excess of construction in numerous markets.

During the economic surge of the late 1970s and early 1980s, developers built an excessive number of new office towers, resulting in an oversupply and a notable decrease in office rents.

While some people ran away from the market, worried about more drops, Zell recognized a chance to purchase troubled office buildings for much less than their original price.

He obtained these assets believing that as the economy improved, the demand for office space would eventually match the surplus supply.

Zell's most well-known use of his contrarian philosophy occurred in the 1990s when he took advantage of the savings and loan industry's downfall.

The crisis, sparked by the collapse of many saving and loan associations, resulted in a surge of foreclosures and distressed sales of real estate assets. The

Resolution Trust Corporation (RTC) was established by the federal government to oversee and sell off these troubled properties.

Zell took advantage of a unique opportunity by buying real estate assets from the RTC at greatly reduced prices.

This action greatly increased his collection of real estate properties and confirmed his status as a "grave dancer" - a title given to him for his skill in making money from troubled situations.

The RTC purchases were risky because a lot of the properties needed major renovations or restructuring. Nevertheless, Zell's readiness to face these difficulties was backed by a distinct plan:

he exclusively put money into properties where he could find a way to enhance value, whether by boosting occupancy, raising rents, or repurposing the asset.

His unique strategy of going against the crowd by purchasing assets during times of selling enabled him to buy assets at low prices with a substantial safety margin.

This plan not only helped to minimize his potential losses but also increased his gains once the market bounced back.

Zell's ideology extended to various industries besides real estate. He implemented a similar contrarian strategy with struggling businesses, acquiring companies that were in trouble or not popular with investors.

He thought that numerous companies faced temporary problems that could be resolved through improvement in management, restructuring, or investment in capital.

Zell's approach to investing in struggling businesses mirrored his strategy for real estate transactions: purchase assets at a reduced price, enhance their performance, and retain them for the foreseeable future.

His readiness to make purchases during market declines, when others lacked courage, enabled him to earn higher-than-average profits on numerous investments.

Sub-chapter 3.2: Risk and Reward: Calculated Decisions

Sam Zell's achievements in investing are not just due to being risky but making careful decisions on which risks to take.

His unconventional strategy often included purchasing troubled assets, but he did it with a thorough comprehension of the associated risks and a well-thought-out plan for handling them.

Zell's method for assessing and controlling risks included extensive research, a methodical decision-making process, and an emphasis on safeguarding against potential losses.

He felt that risk was unavoidable in every investment, but it could be managed and reduced through thorough analysis and strategic planning. One of Zell's key beliefs was the idea of uneven risk-reward balance: he looked for scenarios in which the possible gains were much greater than the possible losses.

When assessing a troubled asset, Zell would consider both its present worth and its future potential in various scenarios.

He sought out investment opportunities that allowed him to add value by enhancing operations, cutting costs, or strategically realigning.

This method enabled him to enhance the chances of a favorable result while reducing his risk of losses. Zell's utilization of leverage also demonstrated his risk management strategies. Although he was willing to use debt for his acquisitions, he made sure not to over-borrow for his investments.

He trusted in keeping a buffer of safety by making sure his properties and businesses could produce enough cash flow to pay their debts, even during challenging market situations.

Utilizing leverage cautiously helped him navigate through recessions and allowed for strategic investments when the market was turbulent.

Another important element of Zell's risk management strategy was his emphasis on maintaining liquidity. He realized that having cash and capital was crucial for survival during market declines. Zell consistently ensured he had enough cash on hand to capitalize on opportunities and handle any unforeseen costs.

This method enabled him to respond promptly to opportunities to purchase distressed assets, frequently outbidding rivals without the necessary financial agility.

Zell's decision to invest in troubled real estate amid the RTC crisis of the early 1990s showcases his deliberate strategy toward balancing risk and reward.

Despite the crisis and abundance of distressed properties on the market, Zell viewed it as a chance to purchase top-notch assets at greatly reduced prices, unlike many other investors. Nevertheless, he did not simply purchase every available property without consideration.

Rather than that, he specifically picked assets with robust fundamentals like prime locations and sturdy buildings, even though they were currently undervalued because of the market circumstances.

His skill in differentiating between assets facing short-term challenges and those with enduring structural issues enabled him to make lucrative investments while reducing risk.

Zell's risk-reward strategy extended beyond just real estate. He implemented the same strategies in different areas such as energy, transportation, and manufacturing. As an example, during the late 1990s, he devoted substantial funds to the energy industry, specifically focusing on natural gas.

During that period, the industry experienced a decrease in prices and changes in regulations, causing numerous investors to avoid it.

However, Zell perceived a chance to purchase energy assets at a reduced price, expecting that prices would go up in the future because of growing demand and restricted supply.

His energy investments were highly profitable when market conditions got better, once again showing his knack for turning well-thought-out risks into significant gains. Zell's capacity to assess risk is also applied to his leadership within the organization.

He surrounded himself with talented experts who shared his investment beliefs and could assist in handling the intricacies of his varied portfolio.

Zell's team played a key role in performing extensive research on possible investments, evaluating market patterns, and implementing recovery plans for struggling assets.

By working together, he was able to utilize his team's skills and make well-informed choices. Nevertheless, not all investments were successful, and Zell experienced setbacks too. In 2008, he encountered major obstacles when his widely known leveraged buyout of the Tribune Company, a large media conglomerate, failed amid the Great Recession, leading to bankruptcy.

The Tribune transaction, which included substantial borrowing, was a departure from Zell's typical strategy of keeping a cushion of security.

The media industry was greatly impacted by the economic recession, causing the company to experience a sharp decline in revenues that made it unable to pay off its debt.

The Tribune experience served as a humble reminder that even well-thought-out risks could fail. However, Zell saw failures as chances to learn. He admitted that despite the deal not going as expected, the situation highlighted the significance of sticking to his investment principles, especially concerning leverage and industry basics.

The setback from Tribune did not stop him from exploring other opportunities, but it did influence his strategy for future investments, stressing the importance of being flexible and adaptable in shifting markets.

In his career, Zell has consistently maintained a balance between boldness and caution in his approach to risk and reward. He was ready to face important risks, but only if he could see a definite way to create value and had a strategy for handling possible negative outcomes.

His skill in handling complicated and unpredictable markets, along with his tendency to go against the crowd, has enabled him to consistently turn obstacles into chances, positioning him as one of the most accomplished investors of his era.

The Zell standard, identified later, was not focused on evading risk but on smartly accepting it.

Zell's career provides important lessons for aspiring entrepreneurs and investors about the significance of recognizing the real essence of risk, critically assessing opportunities and being ready to take action swiftly when the odds are favorable. Sam Zell achieved remarkable success in both real estate and business by purchasing when others were selling and making strategic decisions.

CHAPTER 4

EXPANDING THE EMPIRE

Sub-chapter 4.1: Diversification Beyond Real Estate

Sam Zell's success in the investment industry was not only based on his achievements in real estate but also on his capacity to diversify.

Although real estate was the basis of his wealth, Zell never desired to be limited to just one industry. He advocated for diversification as a way to minimize risk and take advantage of opportunities in various industries.

During his career, Zell actively sought opportunities in various sectors such as energy, transportation, manufacturing, and media. His skill in pinpointing undervalued assets and using his contrarian strategy in different sectors allowed him to create a vast empire that extended well beyond conventional real estate.

Zell believed that various industries have distinct cycles and characteristics, which sparked his interest in diversification.

By spreading investments across various industries, he could take advantage of opportunities in one sector while reducing risk by being involved in others.

His real estate investments were based on principles such as identifying undervalued assets, increasing value through operational changes, and market timing, which he also applied to investments in other industries. He looked for companies with strong foundational qualities that were briefly unpopular or required reorganization.

His strategy involved purchasing these companies for less money, enhancing their functions, and retaining them until they reached their full potential.

Zell made major strides in the energy sector. He started putting money into energy assets in the 1980s, specifically focusing on the oil and natural gas sectors.

In times when energy prices are low, numerous businesses in the industry experienced financial challenges, presenting investment opportunities for individuals such as Zell who had the resources and willingness to purchase troubled assets.

Frequently, he focused on natural gas pipelines and other energy infrastructure, understanding their importance to the economy and the enduring value they held, despite temporary price changes.

Zell's investments carried risk due to the volatile energy sector, but his skill in timing purchases led to substantial gains when market conditions improved.

Furthermore, Zell also ventured into transportation, specifically the railroad sector, alongside his energy ventures. He considered railways to be vital infrastructure with enduring strategic importance, particularly in the United States, where they are still a fundamental method of transporting goods.

In the early 1990s, Zell started buying shares in railway companies that were either going through restructuring or facing operational challenges.

He thought that the industry's economic basics, such as the necessity of moving goods efficiently over long distances, would spur future expansion.

Zell aimed to obtain these companies, enhance their effectiveness and management methods, and ultimately boost their profitability. His focus on creating long-term value in the sector distinguished his investments from those driven by short-term gains. Zell's fascination with media was another important step in diversification.

He acknowledged that despite the fast-changing media environment caused by technological advancements and changes in consumer behavior, there were still chances to create value, especially in struggling traditional media assets.

In 2007, he made a significant media investment by spearheading a leveraged buyout of the Tribune Company, a large newspaper and broadcasting conglomerate.

The agreement, worth more than $8 billion, was among the most ambitious he had ever undertaken in his career. Zell made the company private and assumed the role of chairman, aiming to revive the business in the face of a declining print media industry.

Regrettably, Zell's investment in the Tribune turned out to be one of his toughest ventures.

The agreement happened at the same time as the beginning of the Great Recession, causing a significant negative effect on the advertising income of traditional media platforms.

The Tribune Company faced difficulties due to its debt burden, leading to its bankruptcy filing in 2008. Zell found the failure of the Tribune investment to be a humbling experience, and he later admitted that he had underestimated the deal's complexity and the industry's challenges.

Nevertheless, he saw it as an opportunity for growth rather than a hindrance that shaped his professional journey.

Despite the difficulties faced in the media industry, Zell persisted in his belief in diversification as a fundamental aspect of his investment approach.

Zell applied his diversified investment strategy to various sectors such as healthcare, manufacturing, and retail.

He viewed diversification as more than just risk reduction, also saw it as a way to expand his understanding of various industries and discover fresh investment chances. His skill in transitioning between industries and implementing his unconventional investment approach in various areas showcased his flexibility and grasp of core business concepts.

Zell's main goal, whether investing in energy pipelines, railroads, media companies, or manufacturing plants, was always to seek out value and drive growth through strategic enhancements and timing.

Sub-chapter 4.2: Global Reach: Investing Overseas

While growing his business, Sam Zell started to focus more on international opportunities rather than just domestic ones within the United States.

He understood that investment opportunities were not limited to local markets and that global expansion could provide unique benefits like access to new growth markets, revenue diversification, and exposure to different economic cycles.

He applied the same principles to his global investments as he did to his local projects: discovering assets undervalued, enhancing management, and profiting from timing in the market.

Zell's strategy for global investment included more than just spreading investments across regions, but also comprehending the cultural, regulatory, and economic variations in every market. Zell's initial major investment abroad occurred in the 1990s when he started investing in Latin America.

He viewed the area as ready for investment because of economic changes, privatizing government assets, and an expanding middle class.

One of his main investments was in the telecommunications industry, purchasing shares in companies expanding their networks to keep up with growing demand.

Zell's investments in Latin America were characterized by a concentration on infrastructure and fundamental services, as he anticipated high demand with the growth of the region's economies.

His strategy for investing in Latin America involved teaming up with indigenous companies that had a thorough grasp of the market, reducing the potential risks of investing in unknown regions.

Europe was a significant area of interest for Zell's worldwide growth. During the 2000s, he capitalized on the cyclical nature of the European real estate market, specifically in nations such as the United Kingdom and Germany.

Zell was attracted to markets in which asset prices were disrupted by economic uncertainties or political events. For example, he heavily invested in real estate in Germany after the reunification of East and West Germany, when the country was going through economic changes.

He bought office buildings, retail centers, and other commercial properties that were underestimated because of market uncertainties but had the potential for strong long-term growth.

Zell expanded his investment portfolio beyond developed markets, also delving into emerging economies like China, India, and Southeast Asia.

These markets posed distinctive obstacles, such as regulatory intricacies, currency uncertainties, and varying business methods. Nonetheless, Zell recognized the possibility of substantial profits resulting from fast economic development, urbanization, and rising consumer expenditures.

In China, he concentrated on developing real estate in second-tier cities with industrial growth and an increasing middle class.

Zell positioned his investments for long-term growth by focusing on markets that were developing but had strong economic foundations.

For Zell to invest abroad, he had to adjust his tactics to fit the specific conditions of the local market.

In contrast to his approach in the United States, involving direct management of properties and companies, his international investments often included collaboration with local firms for better market insight.

This cooperative method helped him better overcome regulatory obstacles, cultural variances, and operational difficulties.

Zell thought that collaborating with experts from the local area was essential in reducing the risks linked to global investments while using their expertise to drive growth.

Zell's approach to expanding globally also involved prioritizing liquidity and flexibility. He knew that global markets can be unpredictable, with conditions changing quickly because of economic, political, or regulatory factors. To control these risks, Zell made sure that his global investments were organized in a manner that permitted a fast exit if needed.

He frequently targeted markets where he could ensure liquidity by investing in easily sellable assets or utilizing deals with efficient exit strategies.

This method allowed him to adapt to evolving market conditions and take advantage of emerging opportunities when they appeared.

Although facing difficulties in international investing, Zell's expansion into global markets played a key role in the growth of his empire.

His talent in finding underpriced assets, handling risks, and adjusting to various market conditions allowed him to create a varied portfolio across several continents and sectors.

Zell's global business endeavors not only increased his income sources but also allowed him to diversify risk among various economies and minimize his reliance on the fluctuations of a single market.

Zell showed that value investing, risk management, and market timing principles worked globally in Latin America, Europe, and Asia.

He saw expanding globally as an inherent continuation of his investment strategy, enabling him to discover new opportunities when the local market got too crowded.

Zell's overseas expansion provided important insights for other investors: the significance of grasping local market dynamics, the benefit of collaborating with local specialists, and the necessity of adaptability in overseeing international investments.

For Sam Zell, diversifying and expanding globally were not just ways to expand his empire, they were fundamental aspects of his investment principles.

By branching out from just real estate and taking advantage of international opportunities, he developed a varied and strong portfolio that could handle economic uncertainties and benefit from growth in any location.

His empire proved the strength of thinking differently, seeking value in various sectors and regions, and daring to venture into unknown territories.

Due to his varied investments and worldwide growth, Zell not only accumulated considerable riches but also established a lasting reputation as an innovative investor who viewed the world as his domain.

CHAPTER 5

NAVIGATING CRISES AND DOWNTURNS

Sub-chapter 5.1: Surviving the 1990s Real Estate Crash

The American real estate market faced a turbulent period in the early 1990s, with a notable downturn posing challenges for experienced investors.

During the difficult times of recession, overbuilding, and increasing interest rates, the real estate industry encountered unprecedented obstacles.

Yet, it was in this chaotic period that Sam Zell displayed his determination and clever decision-making, managing the crisis by anticipating, adjusting, and thinking differently. Zell's experience during the 1990s real estate collapse started with the quick expansion of the market in the late 1980s.

The thriving real estate market attracted numerous investors, resulting in an excess of new construction.

Nevertheless, the beginning of this rapid growth started to weaken due to changes in economic circumstances, resulting in a significant decrease in the need for commercial properties.

In the early 1990s, the market that had once been thriving was in chaos, experiencing a high number of vacancies, a sharp decline in property values, and lenders becoming more strict. Having experience as an investor, Zell had a keen understanding of the cyclicality of real estate.

He realized that market downturns were an intrinsic aspect of its cycle. Instead of giving in to panic, he faced the crisis calmly, examining the situation and recognizing possible chances within the disorder.

His skill in staying composed in stressful situations and making strategic decisions in difficult times made him stand out from his peers, who were frequently held back by fear or reluctance to take risks.

During the economic decline, Zell's main tactic was to use his extensive knowledge of troubled assets.

Despite many investors pulling out of the market, Zell identified a special chance to purchase undervalued properties that had been left behind by others.

He always thought that the ideal moment to invest was when others were scared, and the crash of the 1990s gave him the chance to follow this belief.

Zell's initial strategic decision during the economic downturn was to purchase struggling commercial properties at greatly reduced costs.

He searched the market for assets that were undervalued because of market sentiment, not their underlying worth. He used his broad network and understanding of the market to pinpoint properties with future potential, even if they were currently facing challenges.

This opposing strategy enabled him to acquire a collection of top-notch assets at a greatly reduced cost, setting him up for future expansion once the market bounced back.

Furthermore, Zell excelled in securing advantageous financing terms during this timeframe.

In an attempt to reduce their risk in the declining real estate market, banks were eager to provide better financing terms to motivated buyers. Zell took advantage of this situation, obtaining funding that enabled him to expand his acquisitions even more. His readiness to take strategic risks in a difficult setting allowed him to increase his profits when the market started to recover.

Zell learned important lessons about risk management and the significance of liquidity during the economic downturn of the 1990s. He realized that it was essential to maintain financial flexibility during times of crisis.

Through prudent money management and avoiding taking on too much debt, he successfully navigated the challenges without putting his business at risk. This skill would benefit him in upcoming economic challenges, as he would still focus on liquidity and resilience.

Zell's strategic acquisitions during the downturn started to yield results as the economy began to bounce back in the mid-1990s.

The assets he bought at significant markdowns started to increase in worth, leading to the successful growth of his investment portfolio.

He came out of the 1990s not just unharmed but with a much-improved image as a smart investor who can succeed in tough market situations.

His skill in navigating the real estate crash cemented his position as one of the top figures in the industry and paved the way for future achievements.

Sub-chapter 5.2: The Great Recession: A Strategic Response

The 2008 Great Recession brought a completely different series of challenges for both investors and business leaders.

The economic downturn, sparked by the housing market collapse and the ensuing financial crisis, had a significant effect on international markets, causing widespread uncertainty and volatility.

Sam Zell needed to reassess his strategies and adapt quickly to the market dynamics during the Great Recession, despite his previous successful experiences in navigating downturns. With the bursting of the housing bubble and a rise in foreclosures, numerous investors became anxious, either pulling out of the market or selling off assets at heavily discounted prices.

Zell, on the other hand, acknowledged that this crisis, similar to past declines, offered distinct chances for individuals who were able to look past the current disorder.

His contrary impulses emerged once more, prompting him to search for underpriced assets during the chaos.

One of the initial actions Zell made during the Great Recession was to evaluate the condition of his current investment holdings. He carefully watched how well his properties were doing and pinpointed the ones that were most at risk during the economic downturn.

Zell was practical in his approach to the situation, recognizing that certain assets may take longer to bounce back and that he had to be ready to make tough choices.

Instead of holding onto assets that were not performing well, he actively got rid of them, allowing him to invest in more promising opportunities by freeing up capital.

Zell also sought to take advantage of the struggling real estate market. With prices dropping and competition decreasing, he aimed to purchase properties at substantial markdowns.

His plan included focusing on both residential and commercial properties affected by the recession.

His goal was to pinpoint investments with solid long-term foundations that had only been impacted by temporary market situations.

By adopting a perspective focused on the future, Zell set himself up to take advantage of the upcoming rebound after the economic downturn.

Zell understood the significance of liquidity in the crisis, aside from obtaining distressed assets. He realized that having a solid balance sheet was crucial for managing financial instability.

Zell focused on cash flow and implemented strategies to strengthen his financial stability, guaranteeing his ability to take advantage of opportunities as they came up.

His efficient handling of finances enabled him to stay flexible in a constantly changing environment, putting him in a position to act fast when appealing opportunities arose.

Zell also took advantage of the financial crisis to reassess and enhance his partnerships. He wanted to partner with institutional investors and other industry participants who had similar beliefs and methods in value investing.

Through combining resources and knowledge, Zell managed to increase his influence and obtain bigger assets that he may not have been able to obtain on his own.

These collaborations not only improved his collection but also offered extra assistance and perspectives as they tackled the challenges of the economic downturn as a team.

During the Great Recession, Zell's strategy consistently went against the mainstream.

While numerous investors stayed out of the market, he understood that the fear in the market could present distinct chances for those ready to take calculated risks.

His sharp grasp of the recurrent pattern in real estate enabled him to maintain belief in his investment approach.

During the years that followed the recession, Zell's strategic acquisitions and disciplined approach allowed him to take advantage of the increase in property values as the economy started to improve.

One important lesson that Zell learned from the Great Recession was the significance of being adaptable.

The crisis highlighted the importance of investors being adaptable and attentive to quickly evolving market situations.

Zell understood that although his contrarian tactics had been beneficial in the past, the distinctive difficulties of the

Great Recession demanded a more sophisticated plan. He embraced new ideas and aimed to utilize technology and data analysis to guide his investment choices, understanding that the environment was changing.

After the dust settled and the economy started recovering, Zell's reputation as a smart investor who could succeed during tough times was even stronger coming out of the Great Recession.

His resilience and strategic thinking were demonstrated by his skill in navigating the crisis and recognizing opportunities in a tumultuous setting.

The investments he made during this time would greatly impact his future success, establishing his reputation as a prominent figure in the real estate sector. Zell's encounters during the real estate crash of the 1990s and the Great Recession are important examples for aspiring entrepreneurs and investors.

His capacity to sustain a long-range outlook, navigate risks, and adjust to shifting market conditions underscores the significance of resilience in times of challenge.

Through adopting a contrarian attitude and staying committed to his strategy, Zell not only managed to withstand economic downturns but also transformed them into chances for development and achievement.

In conclusion, dealing with crises and downturns is an unavoidable aspect of investing and business leadership.

Sam Zell's experience navigating the real estate downturns of the 1990s and the Great Recession illustrates how investors can prosper in tough times with strategic thinking, going against the crowd, and being financially disciplined.

His skill in identifying opportunities during difficult times has had a long-lasting effect on the real estate industry, motivating a new wave of entrepreneurs to view challenges as opportunities for achieving success.

CHAPTER 6

LEADERSHIP AND CORPORATE CULTURE

Sub-chapter 6.1: Building Teams: The Importance of Talent and Culture

Sam Zell is a giant in the real estate industry, not just because of his clever investments and unique philosophy but also because of his outstanding skill in creating and guiding teams.

Zell believes that the key to a thriving business is its employees. He strongly believes that recruiting the correct skills and nurturing a business-oriented work atmosphere is vital for any company aspiring to achieve sustained success.

Zell's approach to talent acquisition extends past simply filling roles; it entails recognizing individuals who exemplify the traits and beliefs that align with the company's mission.

He has consistently looked for team members who possess both expertise and a drive for creativity, along with a readiness to embrace strategic risks.

His hiring practices prioritize character, attitude, and growth potential over traditional qualifications.

Zell's companies usually have a thorough selection process that evaluates candidates' skills in adapting, collaborating, and excelling in a high-speed setting. Zell recognizes that having the correct team is crucial for a company's success, and he values people who show initiative and take responsibility.

This belief is based on his personal experiences as a business owner, where he realized the importance of having skilled and inspired people around him who could help achieve the company's goals.

Furthermore, Zell promotes a work environment that motivates employees to think like entrepreneurs no matter their role in the company.

He trusts in giving employees the authority to take control of their tasks, make choices, and explore creative concepts without worrying about making mistakes.

This environment of trust and freedom not only boosts employee involvement but also improves innovation and efficiency.

Zell fosters a workspace that values and respects team members, allowing them to perform at their highest level.

Transparency and open communication are fundamental aspects of Zell's leadership approach. He promotes feedback and conversation in his teams, acknowledging that various perspectives can improve decision-making.

Focusing on communication helps to create a feeling of teamwork among workers, breaking down barriers and encouraging cooperation between different departments.

Zell frequently emphasizes the value of collective intelligence in fostering innovation and reaching shared objectives, and he is dedicated to creating an inclusive environment where every person's input is respected.

Furthermore, Zell's dedication to fostering diversity and inclusion among his teams enhances his company's culture even more.

He recognizes that having a variety of employees with different backgrounds can improve innovation and problem-solving.

Zell encourages diversity by actively seeking out individuals from different backgrounds and promoting various viewpoints, creating an environment where innovation flourishes and employees feel empowered to share their unique perspectives.

Zell has also transformed his leadership approach to include mentorship and growth chances for his teams.

He supports developing skills and committing to the development of his staff, understanding that their achievements are linked to the success of the organization.

The dedication to employee growth is shown in the various training opportunities and resources provided, enabling them to improve their skills and progress in their careers.

Zell's approach to forming teams and nurturing company culture is primarily based on the strong belief in the potential of individuals.

By emphasizing talent recruitment, fostering an entrepreneurial mindset, and promoting transparent communication, he establishes a space where people can thrive and add value to the company's achievements.

This philosophy has not just assisted Zell in creating prosperous businesses, it has also had a long-lasting influence on the industry, motivating others to implement comparable strategies in their own companies.

Sub-chapter 6.2: Leading by Example: The Art of Direct Communication

Sam Zell's leadership philosophy revolves around his unique form of straightforward communication.

He is recognized for his direct method that focuses on honesty, clarity, and straightforwardness in every interaction.

This way of communicating has been crucial in influencing the culture within his companies and promoting trust and respect among his teams.

Zell's leadership style is defined by his readiness to participate in open and honest discussions, whether it be with staff, collaborators, or individuals invested in the organization.

He thinks that having transparency is crucial in developing solid relationships and making sure that everyone is on the same page with the organization's objectives.

This dedication to transparent communication fosters an environment where team members can freely express their thoughts and communicate their ideas without worrying about negative consequences.

Zell's honesty also applies to his approach to giving feedback, whether it is to commend or offer guidance. He doesn't sugarcoat his messages; he prefers to give a candid assessment of performance and behavior.

This method assists employees in knowing their position and offers clear directions for improvement.

Zell promotes continuous growth and development within his teams by cultivating a culture of positive feedback, emphasizing its importance as a beneficial tool for success rather than something to be feared.

Moreover, Zell's focus on clear communication is apparent in both his leadership meetings and company events.

He is recognized for being candid and genuine in these meetings, expressing his beliefs and hopes while also encouraging feedback from others.

This effort establishes transparency and fosters a cooperative environment where team members are motivated to participate in discussions.

Zell knows that when employees feel like their voices are being listened to, they are more likely to be motivated and committed to their tasks.

Zell's straightforward communication approach also applies to handling crises. In difficult circumstances, he thinks that confronting problems directly is the best way to handle uncertainty.

Instead of avoiding tough discussions, he addresses obstacles openly, ensuring his teams are well-informed and involved every step of the way. This degree of transparency not only reduces stress but also builds a feeling of solidarity among workers as they collaborate to conquer challenges.

Furthermore, Zell sets a good example, showing how crucial accountability and integrity are in every business endeavor.

He upholds the same expectations for himself as he does for his teams, and his dedication to ethical behavior influences the entire organization.

Zell fosters a culture of trust by practicing the values he advocates and encouraging employees to do the same.

Zell's leadership approach has enabled him to develop solid connections with investors and business allies. His honesty and openness create trust with stakeholders, making sure they are informed and in agreement with the organization's goals.

This method is advantageous, especially in difficult economic times when effective communication can greatly help in keeping investor trust and confidence.

To summarize, Sam Zell's leadership style and company culture are based on his dedication to forming robust teams and encouraging transparent communication.

His focus on recruiting talented individuals, fostering an entrepreneurial mindset, and promoting open communication has fostered a culture where staff feel appreciated and empowered to make impactful contributions towards the company's achievements. Zell's straightforward leadership style boosts performance and fosters a culture based on trust, cooperation, and responsibility.

Due to Zell's exceptional leadership philosophy, his companies have prospered, overcoming obstacles and taking advantage of opportunities.

CHAPTER 7

THE ZELL LEGACY

Sub-chapter 7.1: Philanthropy and Giving Back

Sam Zell's rise from a modest start in Chicago to achieving billionaire status in the real estate sector is notable, not just for the wealth it brought but also for the philanthropic contributions he has made.

Zell, a prosperous entrepreneur, recognizes the significance of giving back to the communities that have provided him support.

His charitable work showcases his business principles and dedication to creating a positive impact on the world, especially in the areas of education, the arts, and community growth.

The fundamentals of charitable giving

Zell's philanthropic beliefs are based on the idea that education is a crucial asset for empowerment and development.

He acknowledges that quality education access can transform lives and unlock opportunities for people from diverse backgrounds.

During his professional trajectory, Zell has endorsed a range of educational efforts by offering scholarships and financial support to institutions that encourage education and creativity.

An example that stands out of Zell's dedication to education is his participation in the University of Michigan, where he completed his bachelor's degree.

In 2003, he gifted $5 million to create the Zell Founders Fund, designed to assist entrepreneurial studies at the university.

This fund supports new entrepreneurs financially and also gives them mentorship chances, showcasing Zell's belief in the value of hands-on learning and direction for upcoming leaders.

Zell goes beyond just giving money, he also has a philanthropic approach. He frequently engages in activities and programs aimed at motivating and guiding aspiring entrepreneurs.

His goal is to prepare the upcoming generation for the intricate business world by imparting his own experiences and insights.

This active participation shows his dedication to promoting entrepreneurship to drive economic growth and innovation.

Promoting the arts

Zell not only values education but also strongly advocates for the arts. He comprehends the important impact that culture and creativity have on enriching communities and improving quality of life.

Zell has supported several arts institutions, such as the Chicago Symphony Orchestra and the Museum of Contemporary Art.

His backing enables these organizations to flourish and persevere in their goals of promoting artistic creativity and recognition.

Zell's commitment to the arts goes beyond financial support; it showcases his faith in the ability of creativity to encourage transformation and unite individuals.

He acknowledges that the arts have the potential to spark conversation and comprehension, promoting unity and collective involvement.

Zell's goal is to guarantee that upcoming generations have the opportunity to engage in cultural experiences that will expand their horizons and inspire their creativity.

Efforts to enhance the development of local communities

Zell also concentrates his philanthropic work on developing and rejuvenating communities.

He strongly values the significance of investing in communities to develop sustainable and prosperous environments for individuals and families.

Zell has contributed to supporting affordable housing projects, economic development programs, and local business growth through a range of initiatives.

His dedication is evident in his participation in revitalizing neglected areas in Chicago. Zell's investments in projects aiming to rejuvenate these neighborhoods create opportunities for residents by improving access to necessary services and enhancing quality of life. He recognizes the importance of thriving communities for personal health and financial prosperity.

Zell doesn't just donate money, he also makes an effort to connect with communities and learn about their specific struggles and requirements.

This practical method enables him to customize his projects for maximum impact, making sure resources are used wisely and efficiently.

Matching charitable giving with corporate beliefs.

Zell's charitable giving is in line with his business principles, mirroring his conviction in the significance of honesty, responsibility, and involvement in the community.

He applies the same strategic approach to his philanthropic endeavors as he does to his business ventures.

By concentrating on projects that promote long-term development and give people control, he aims to make a lasting difference that goes beyond just financial donations.

Moreover, Zell also recognizes that philanthropy involves more than just donating money, but also creating an environment supportive of charitable actions. He advises other corporate executives to engage with their local communities and back projects that align with their beliefs.

Zell aims to motivate a new wave of entrepreneurs to incorporate philanthropy into their business endeavors by setting a good example.

Overall, Sam Zell's lasting impact is marked by a sincere dedication to charitable acts and supporting the community.

By contributing to education, the arts, and community development, he strives to bring about positive change and enable individuals to achieve their maximum potential. Zell exemplifies how success is defined by both financial achievement and the impact on the world, inspiring aspiring entrepreneurs to align philanthropy with business values.

Sub-chapter 7.2: The Blueprint for Future Entrepreneurs

Sam Zell's impressive journey in real estate and investing provides valuable lessons for those wanting to start their businesses.

His voyage demonstrates the strength of resilience, strategic planning, and the readiness to take calculated risks. Reflecting on his experiences, Zell identifies important principles that can assist aspiring entrepreneurs in finding success on their journeys.

Adopting a mindset that goes against the norm.

An essential lesson from Zell's career is the value of embracing a contrarian outlook.

During his journey, he has continuously stressed the importance of thinking in ways that differ from the majority.

While some investors may run away during tough times or steer clear of potential risks, Zell has prospered by searching for underpriced assets in difficult markets.

This opposing strategy demands a profound comprehension of market trends, the capability to assess opportunities rigorously, and the bravery to take action in the face of others' indecision.

Zell urges future entrepreneurs to cultivate their distinctive viewpoints and not shy away from questioning traditional beliefs.

In this way, they are able to spot opportunities that could be missed by others, resulting in creative solutions and possibly profitable endeavors.

Gain knowledge from mistakes.

Failure is an unavoidable aspect of every entrepreneurial endeavor, and Zell is familiar with challenges. He stresses the significance of gaining knowledge from failures and seeing them as beneficial experiences instead of obstacles. Zell sees every mistake as a chance to learn and improve, making failure a necessary aspect of the learning journey.

Those looking to start their businesses should adopt a mentality of perseverance, recognizing that challenges do not determine their ability to succeed.

Instead of dwelling on their mistakes, they should evaluate the errors, amend their tactics, and continue with a stronger resolve. Zell's long-term success can be attributed to his ability to bounce back from difficulties, highlighting the importance of persistence.

Place relationships as a top priority.

In the business realm, relationships are priceless. Zell has established his professional success through strong relationships with partners, investors, and colleagues.

He stresses the significance of building a strong network and forming valuable relationships, as these connections can lead to new opportunities and offer assistance in times of difficulty.

Zell advises potential entrepreneurs to focus on creating strong relationships and dedicating time and energy to connecting with like-minded individuals who have similar values and objectives.

By forming a robust support system with mentors and peers, they can receive valuable knowledge, exchange stories, and work together on cutting-edge initiatives.

Remain flexible and quick to respond

The business environment is always changing, and entrepreneurs need to be flexible in order to succeed.

Zell has experienced different market changes and economic fluctuations in his career, highlighting the significance of being adaptable in addressing change.

He stresses the importance of keeping up-to-date on industry trends, customer preferences, and new technologies in order to stay competitive.

Entrepreneurs who are aiming for success should develop a flexible mindset, enabling them to adapt when needed and take advantage of emerging opportunities.

By remaining aware of the trends in their markets, they can set themselves up for success even when faced with uncertainty.

Promote an environment that encourages creativity and new ideas.

Zell's leadership style is strongly focused on creating an environment of innovation in his companies.

He thinks that promoting creativity and taking risks at every level is necessary for sustainable growth in the long run.

Zell has created a setting where employees are encouraged to share ideas and try new things, leading to ongoing improvement and flexibility.

Encouraging their teams to think creatively and explore new approaches is key for aspiring entrepreneurs looking to cultivate a culture of innovation.

By appreciating various viewpoints and promoting teamwork, they have the opportunity to unlock innovative ideas that can set their businesses apart in competitive industries.

Emphasize creating value.

Zell's investment philosophy is centered on a dedication to creating value. He stresses the significance of grasping customer requirements and providing products or services that truly improve their quality of life. Entrepreneurs can achieve long-term success by prioritizing value and cultivating strong customer loyalty.

Entrepreneurs in training should embrace a customer-focused approach, constantly gathering feedback and information to improve their products or services.

By putting value creation ahead of immediate profits, companies can create a lasting business model that connects with customers.

Dedicate yourself to continuous learning throughout your life.

Zell's professional trajectory is marked by a dedication to ongoing learning and development.

He acknowledges that the business environment constantly changes and that staying ahead necessitates continuous learning and growth.

Zell highlights the significance of pursuing knowledge and adjusting to new information, whether it be through schooling, guidance, or personal learning.

Prospective business owners must adopt a mentality of continuous learning, staying curious, and receptive to fresh ideas. Investing in their personal and professional growth will provide them with the necessary skills and knowledge to navigate the challenges of entrepreneurship effectively.

Contribute to the Community

In conclusion, Zell's impact emphasizes the significance of contributing to the community.

He thinks that it is important for successful entrepreneurs to give back to society in a positive way, whether by donating money, mentoring others, or getting involved in the community.

Entrepreneurs can have a significant influence and motivate others by giving back through initiatives that support their communities.

Those aiming to start their own businesses should think about incorporating social responsibility into their business plans, understanding that success is measured not just by profits but also by the impact they have on society.

Final thoughts

Future generations can learn valuable lessons from Sam Zell's successful entrepreneurial journey and rise to billionaire status.

Zell has set the path for hopeful entrepreneurs to navigate their paths by having a contrarian mindset, resilience in failure, emphasis on relationships, adaptability, commitment to innovation, focus on creating value, dedication to lifelong learning, and a strong sense of social responsibility. By adopting these principles, upcoming entrepreneurs can pave their way to success, taking guidance from Zell's impressive career and legacy.

As they start their entrepreneurial ventures, they will discover that creating a lasting impact depends not just on their business success, but also on the positive difference they make in society and the people they influence.

Zell's voyage demonstrates that real success is determined by the impact one has on others, inspiring future generations to dream big and act boldly, and leaving behind a meaningful legacy.

www.ingramcontent.com/pod-product-compliance
Lightning Source LLC
Chambersburg PA
CBHW050305230526
45471CB00005B/2032